Guinea Pigs

by Martha E. H. Rustad

Consulting Editor: Gail Saunders-Smith, Ph.D.

Consultant: Jennifer Zablotny, D.V.M.,
Member, American Animal Hospital Association

Pebble Books

an imprint of Capstone Press
Mankato, Minnesota

Pebble Books are published by Capstone Press
151 Good Counsel Drive, P.O. Box 669, Mankato, Minnesota 56002
http://www.capstone-press.com

1 2 3 4 5 6 07 06 05 04 03 02

Library of Congress Cataloging-in-Publication Data
Rustad, Martha E. H. (Martha Elizabeth Hillman), 1975–
    Guinea pigs / by Martha E. H. Rustad.
    p. cm.—(All about pets)
    Includes bibliographical references (p. 23) and index.
    ISBN 0-7368-0975-9
    1. Guinea pigs as pets—Juvenile literature. [1. Guinea pigs. 2. Pets.] I. Title.
II. All about pets (Mankato, Minn.)
SF459.G9 R87 2002
636.9'3592—dc21   2001000258

Summary: Simple text and photographs introduce and illustrate pet guinea pigs,
their features, and basic care.

Note to Parents and Teachers

The All About Pets series supports national science standards for units on the diversity and unity of life. This book describes guinea pigs and illustrates what they need from their owners. The photographs support emergent readers in understanding the text. The repetition of words and phrases helps emergent readers learn new words. This book also introduces emergent readers to subject-specific vocabulary words, which are defined in the Words to Know section. Emergent readers may need assistance to read some words and to use the Table of Contents, Words to Know, Read More, Internet Sites, and Index/Word List sections of the book.

Table of Contents

Guinea pigs are pets.

paws

Guinea pigs have paws.

Some guinea pigs
have long fur.

Some guinea pigs
have short fur.

Guinea pigs need
to be brushed often.

Guinea pigs need food and water.

Guinea pigs need
a clean cage.

bedding

Guinea pigs need
clean bedding.

Guinea pigs need room to play.

Words to Know

bedding—something used to make a bed; guinea pigs use wood shavings, straw, and shredded paper for bedding.

brush—to smooth hair or fur using an object with bristles and a handle; pet owners should brush guinea pigs' fur a few times each week.

cage—a container that holds an animal; a guinea pig needs a cage with a solid floor so its small feet do not get stuck in the cage.

food—something that people, animals, and plants need to stay alive; guinea pigs eat guinea pig food pellets and some fruits and vegetables.

fur—the soft, thick, hairy coat of an animal; the fur of guinea pigs can be brown, gray, white, or black.

paw—the foot of an animal; most animals with paws have four feet and claws; pet owners should clip guinea pigs' claws when they get too long.

Read More

Head, Honor. *Guinea Pig.* My Pet. Austin, Texas: Raintree Steck-Vaughn, 2001.

Hughes, Sarah. *My Guinea Pig.* My Pet. New York : Children's Press, 2000.

Miller, Michaela. *Guinea Pigs.* Pets. Des Plaines, Ill.: Heinemann Interactive Library, 1998.

Internet Sites

Critter Collection: Cavy
http://animalnetwork.com/critters/profiles/cavy/default.asp

Guinea Pig Care and Feeding
http://www.healthypet.com/Library/care-23.html

The Guinea Pig Club
http://www.petclubhouse.com/guineapig

Index/Word List

bedding, 19
brushed, 13
cage, 17
clean, 17, 19
food, 15
fur, 9, 11
long, 9
need, 13, 15, 17,
19, 21

often, 13
paws, 7
pets, 5
play, 21
room, 21
short, 11
some, 9, 11
water, 15

Word Count: 50
Early-Intervention Level: 6

Credits
Kia Bielke, cover designer and illustrator; Kimberly Danger, photo researcher

Capstone Press/Gary Sundermeyer, cover, 6, 12, 14 (both), 16, 18, 20
International Stock/George Ancona, 4
Ken Schwab/Photo Agora, 8
Photri-Microstock, 1
Unicorn Stock Photos/Ted Rose, 10

Special thanks to Pet Expo in Mankato, Minnesota, for their help with photo shoots for this book. Guinea pigs provided by Pet Expo, Mankato, Minnesota.